THE STORY OF SIMONE BILES

A Biography Book for New Readers

Written by
Rachelle Burk

Illustrated by
Steffi Walthall

ROCKRIDGE
PRESS

For Corrie—when you put your mind to it, you can do anything.

Series Designer: Angela Navarra
Interior and Cover Designer: Scott Petrower
Art Producer: Hannah Dickerson
Editor: Kristen Depken
Production Editor: Mia Moran

Illustrations © 2020 Steffi Walthall. Photography © PCN Photography/Alamy Stock Photo, pp. 48, 49; Leonard Zhukovsky/Shutterstock, p. 51. All maps used under license from Creative Market. Author photo courtesy of Alana Barouch. Illustrator photo courtesy of Clarence Goss.

ISBN: Print 978-1-64739-775-3 | eBook 978-1-64739-462-2
R0
Printed in China

CONTENTS

CHAPTER 1
AN OLYMPIAN IS BORN

Meet Simone

In 2016, the whole world was watching Simone Biles **compete** in the **Olympics**. To try to relax, Simone told herself that this was just like **gymnastics** practice. But it wasn't practice. It was the biggest sports contest in the world. Simone had prepared her entire life for this moment. Even though she felt nervous, she wanted to have fun. She waved to the crowd and flashed her famous smile. Then she performed a near-perfect gymnastics **routine**.

Simone Biles has been called the best **gymnast** in the world. Her **training** began before anyone realized it. As a child, Simone did backflips off mailboxes and swings. She scrambled up her big brothers' backs and did pull-ups on their outstretched arms. Simone was a ball of energy! No one imagined she would one day win more gymnastics awards than anyone in history.

Simone's life has not always been easy. She was born into **poverty**. She has had hard days and disappointments. But Simone believed in herself, worked hard, and did not give up. As a result, she soared to great heights.

Simone's World

Simone was born in Columbus, Ohio, on March 14, 1997. When she was three, she moved to Texas, where her life as a gymnast began.

Gymnastics is a very challenging sport. Gymnasts must develop powerful muscles. They also need **flexibility**, **balance**, and **agility** to perform difficult skills. Some gymnasts leave the sport because it takes so much hard work. Others leave due to injuries. Not Simone! She practiced for hours every day. She wanted to be a top gymnast and enter **championships** around the world. Simone also dreamed of going to the Olympics one day.

MYTH & FACT

MYTH: Women have always competed in the Olympics.

FACT: Female athletes were not allowed to compete in any Olympic events until 1900.

The Olympics are a series of sports **competitions** held in a different country every four years since 1896. The **athletes** who compete there are the very best in their sports.

At the Olympics, medals are awarded to the best athletes in each event. First-place medals are gold, second-place are silver, and third-place are bronze. For many years, there were only a few American Olympic medal winners for young female gymnasts to look up to. In 1984, Mary Lou Retton was the first American woman to win an individual gold medal in gymnastics. In 1996, just six months before Simone was born, the

United States women's gymnastics team won its first gold medal in the team competition. Simone was too young to compete in the 2012 Olympics, but she watched as the United States women's team won three gold medals! It was an exciting time in women's gymnastics, and Simone had many heroes to admire. Before long, she would compete with some of them!

WHEN?

1984 — Mary Lou Retton wins Olympic gold.

1996 — The US women's gymnastics team wins gold.

1997 — Simone is born on March 14 in Columbus, Ohio.

CHAPTER 2

THE EARLY YEARS

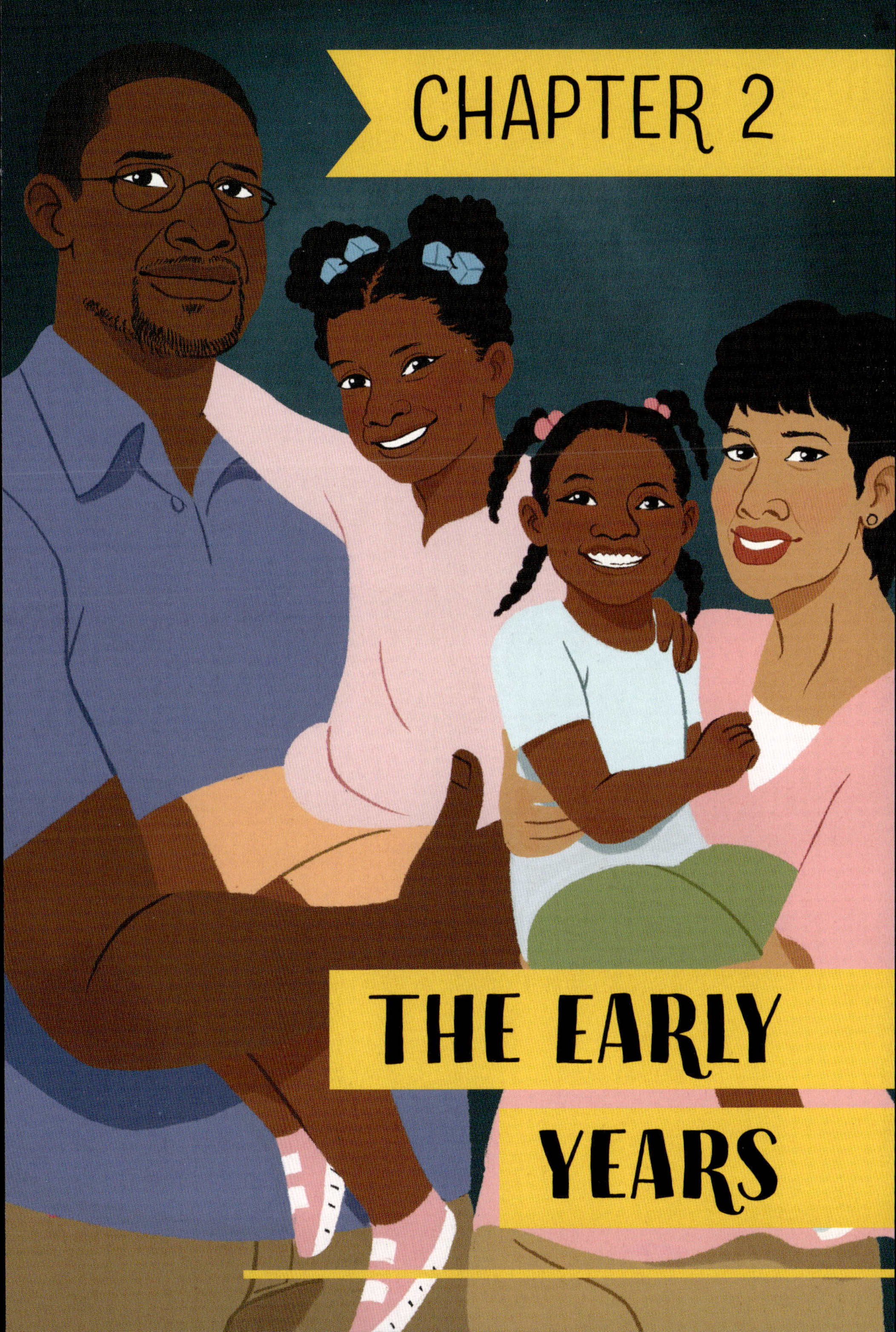

From Ohio to Texas

When Simone was a baby, she lived in Ohio with her mom, Shanon, and three siblings. Ashley and Tevin were older than Simone, and Adria was younger. Sadly, Shanon was unable to take good care of the four children. When Simone was three years old, she and her siblings were

placed in **foster care**. They lived with a kind family who took care of them and tried to keep them safe. However, when no one was looking, Simone would climb onto countertops and into her little sister's crib. She flew high on the swing set and leaped off in midair. She longed to jump on her foster family's trampoline, but they said she was too small.

Eventually, Ashley and Tevin were **adopted** by a relative in Ohio. Simone and Adria went to live with their grandparents, Ronald and Nellie, in Spring, Texas. When Simone was six, her grandparents adopted her and Adria.

MYTH & FACT

MYTH: Gymnastics is just a girls' sport.

FACT: Anyone can practice gymnastics. In fact, gymnastics was invented by ancient Greeks for men to show off strength and bravery.

From that day on, Grandma and Grandpa became Mom and Dad. Simone's teenage uncles, Adam and Ronnie, became her new big brothers.

Simone's new home in Texas was happy and full of love. It even had a trampoline in the backyard! Simone felt so happy that she never stopped smiling. She bounced and flipped for hours, practicing skills she would use later in gymnastics.

The Biles Family

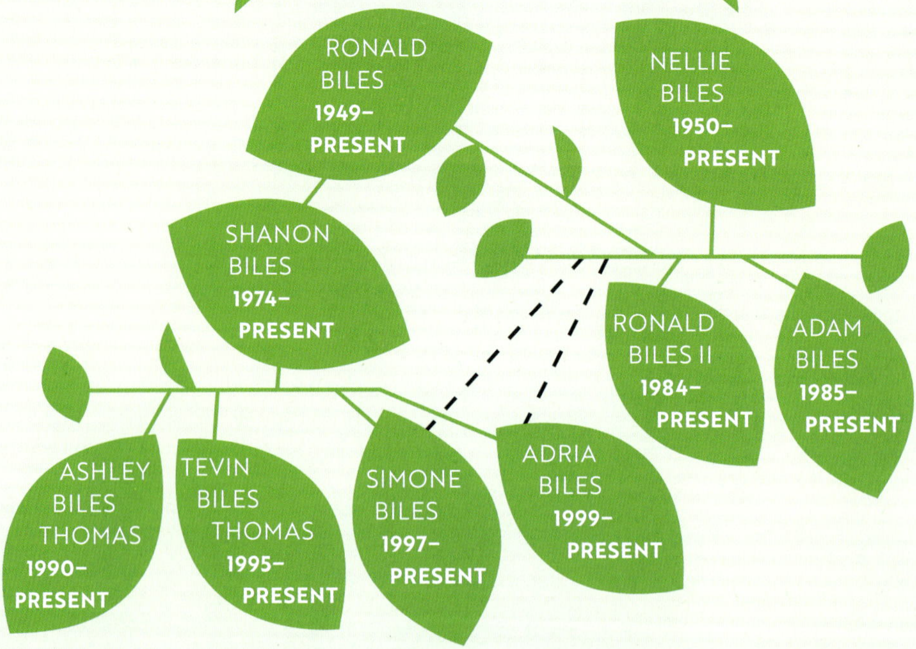

A New Interest

Simone was a bubbly little girl with a lot of energy. When she was six years old, she went on a field trip to a gymnastics center. She loved it!

Simone watched the older gymnasts and tried to copy their jumps and backflips. A coach at the gym saw Simone and thought she had talent. She invited Simone to sign up for classes. Her mother agreed that gymnastics would be a good way for Simone to use some of her energy. She signed Simone and Adria up for classes.

JUMP -IN THE- THINK TANK

Everyone has skills and talents. What are the things you do well? What would you need to do to get even better?

At the gym, Simone was fearless and loved to show off. She wore bright, sparkly **leotards**. She could spin through the air as well as the older gymnasts. When asked to do five push-ups, she did 10. If she was told to climb 10 feet up a rope, she climbed 20. She wanted to prove that even though she was small, she was powerful.

Simone soon joined the **junior elite** program, which trains young gymnasts to move up through 10 levels of difficulty. There are four main skills in women's gymnastics: the **uneven bars**, the **vault**, the **balance beam**, and **floor exercise**. Moving up means getting better and better at each skill. Simone moved up quickly. By the time she was eight years old, she had reached level seven. She was ready to learn more difficult routines.

WHEN?

1999 Simone's sister Adria is born.

1999 Simone and her siblings are put in foster care.

2000 Simone and Adria move to Texas.

2003 Simone and Adria are adopted by their grand-parents.

2003 Simone begins gymnastics classes.

CHAPTER 3

BALANCING ACT

A New Routine

Of the four gymnastics skills, Simone loved the floor exercise most. She was also very good at balancing on the beam and springing from the vault. But the uneven bars were her biggest challenge. She was short for her age, and her hands were small. This made circling, catching, and swinging between the bars difficult for her. When she took a bad fall, she was terrified to get back on. Still, her coaches wouldn't let her give up.

Every day after school, Simone practiced for four hours at the gym with Coach Aimee Boorman. Within three years, Simone soared to level nine. By age 11, Simone was winning competitions against much older gymnasts.

At home, Simone wanted a dog. Her father told her that they could finally get one if Simone scored high enough at an upcoming contest.

She won first place on floor and second in **all-around**, an event that combines all four skills. Soon after that, Simone came home with a German shepherd puppy named Maggie.

To go as far as she could as a gymnast, Simone needed more time to practice. For eighth grade, she enrolled in a private school near the gym so she could train before and after school. The new school was not a happy place for Simone. She felt that she did not fit in well with the other students. She couldn't concentrate on her schoolwork. A doctor told Simone she had **ADHD**. She started taking medication that helped her focus.

It was a tough school year, but it meant Simone had 10 extra hours every week to train. She made good friends at the gym. That was her place to let loose, laugh, and burn off energy.

JUMP —IN THE— THINK TANK

Have you ever felt so frustrated with a task that you wanted to give up? What kept you going?

A Big Decision

Coach Aimee told Simone to always do her best. She also said that training and competing should be fun. Now at level 10, Simone had big dreams of going **elite**. Only the very best become elite gymnasts. They compete at national and world competitions as part of the national team.

At the 2011 USA Gymnastics National Championships, Simone wanted to win a spot on the national team. She did her best but missed making the team by only one spot. Simone smiled and clapped for the winners. When she was alone, she sobbed. She would have to work longer and harder to make the team.

Simone was about to start high school and wanted to go to a regular school with her friends. But if she did that, she wouldn't have enough time for the extra training she needed. The only way she could put in more hours at the gym was to be **homeschooled** instead. Simone had a difficult decision to make. She could only follow one

of her dreams—going elite or having a normal high school life. She asked her parents what to do, but they said it was her choice to make. It was the hardest decision of her life. She decided to be homeschooled.

> "I don't think about size—I focus more on being powerful and confident!"

WHEN?

2005	2008	2011	2012
Aimee Boorman becomes Simone's coach.	Simone gets a puppy named Maggie.	Simone fails to make the national team.	Simone begins home-schooling.

CHAPTER 4

BECOMING A CHAMPION

The Elite Life

Homeschooling allowed Simone to train at the gym for more than five hours a day. Even though she wanted to become a better gymnast, she didn't like missing out on the fun things her friends were doing in high school. Sometimes she felt sad and confused. She often cried and snapped at her family. Her parents were patient. So was Coach Aimee. They helped Simone stay focused on her goals.

Simone began extra training with Márta Károlyi, a famous coach who had worked with many Olympic gymnasts. Simone practiced difficult routines from morning until night. Her efforts paid off. In 2012, Simone finally made the junior national team! That summer, Simone watched the Olympic Games on TV, cheering as the United States women's gymnastics team won gold and silver medals. She imagined that she could one day be an Olympic champion, too.

When Simone turned 16, she became a **senior elite** gymnast. She began competing against gymnastics champions she had looked up to for years, such as Gabby Douglas, Aly Raisman, and Kyla Ross. She wasn't sure if she was good enough. At an important meet, Simone felt anxious and unprepared. She stumbled on the balance beam. She fell off the high bar.

She crashed on her floor routine and hurt her ankle. Coach Aimee took her out of the competition. Simone worried that her gymnastics dreams were coming to a sudden end.

> "I proved to myself that I could do things that I didn't think I could."

Taking On the World

Simone met with a **sports psychologist** to talk about her feelings. She told him she felt pressure to succeed and worried about disappointing people. She was not having fun anymore. Over many meetings, the psychologist helped Simone see that she only needed to do her best and have a good time. She started feeling strong and confident again. Later that year, she became the all-around national champion. That meant she

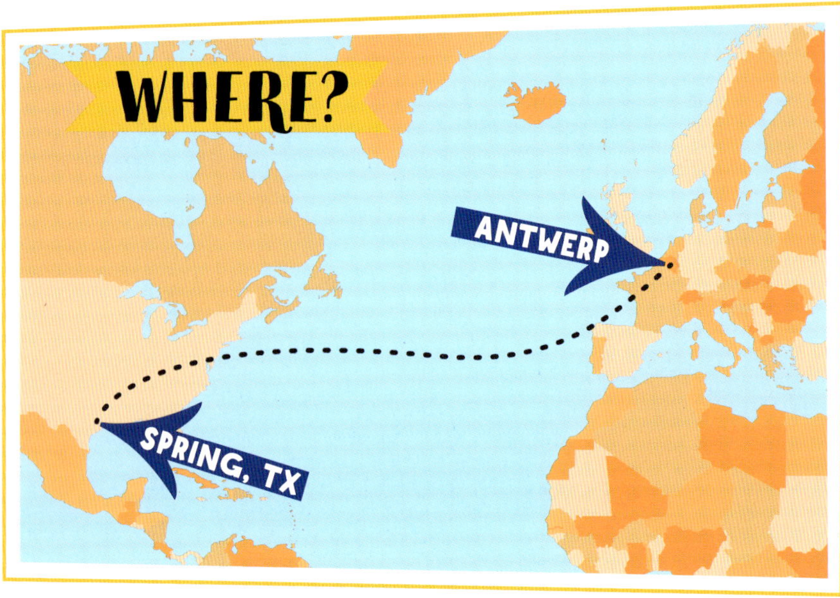

was the best gymnast in the country in all four skills. Simone was the first Black American to win that **title**. Best of all, she was having fun again!

At her first **world championship** in Antwerp, Belgium, Simone showed off a daring new move in her floor routine. It was a difficult double flip with a half twist landing that became known as the Biles. She won the all-around gold medal. Within two years, Simone set a new record for the most world championship medals ever won in women's gymnastics.

In the sports world, Simone was a superstar. At home, she was just an ordinary teenager.

JUMP –IN THE– THINK TANK

When Simone felt discouraged, it helped her to talk to someone. Who do you like to talk to when you have a problem?

She did chores, hung out with her friends, and played with her dogs. When she got her driver's license, her parents bought her a car. They wanted her to know that a car comes with responsibilities, so they told her she would have to drive her sister to school every day. Even though that meant waking up an hour earlier each day, Simone loved having her own car! To help with Simone's busy schedule, her parents made plans to build their own gym close to home. The Biles family opened the World Champions Centre in Spring, Texas, in 2016.

WHEN?

The US women's gymnastics team wins gold.

2012

Simone earns a spot on the junior national team.

2012

Simone is pulled from the US Secret Classic Competition.

2013

Simone wins gold in her first world championship.

2013

The World Champions Centre opens.

2016

CHAPTER 5

MAKING THE TEAM

Going Pro

When Simone graduated from high school, she had to make another hard decision about her **education**. She had always planned on going to **college**. She wanted to learn alongside other students and have fun with her classmates, something she missed during her high school years. College gymnastics coaches from all over the country invited her to join their teams. But that would mean giving up her Olympic dream and the chance to go pro.

Going pro, or **professional**, would mean Simone would get paid to do what she loved most—gymnastics. Many companies pay top athletes to **promote** their products, such as sports clothing and breakfast cereals. As one of the top gymnasts in the country, Simone could earn a lot of money. However, professional athletes are not allowed to compete in college

JUMP IN THE THINK TANK

We never know what we can do until we try. What have you believed you couldn't do but then succeeded at?

sports. If Simone went pro, she could not be a college gymnast. Simone asked her parents and her sister what to do. Should she give up college life or her Olympic dreams? Simone's family could not make the decision for her. She had to choose her own path. Simone decided to delay college and focus on the 2016 Olympics.

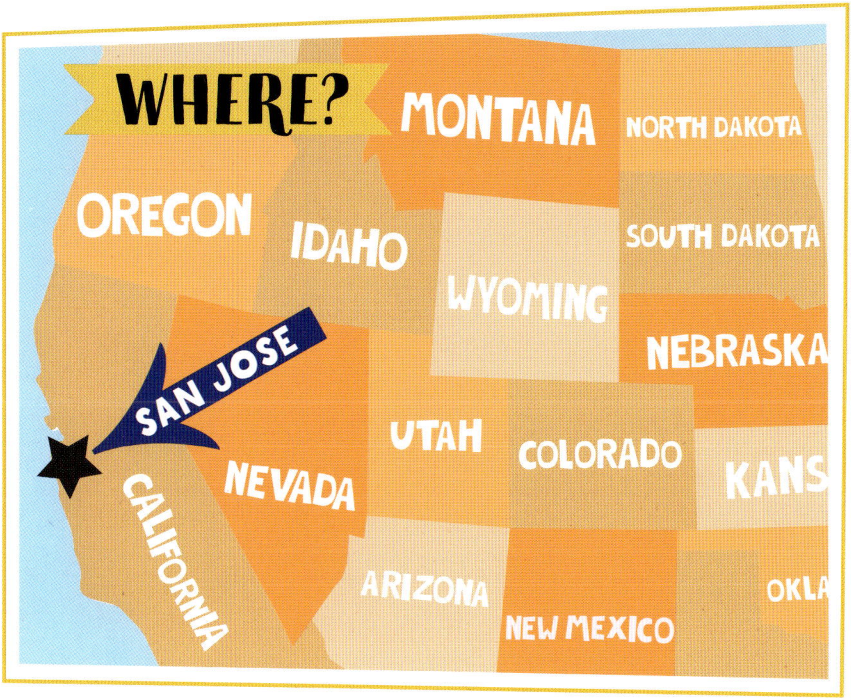

☆ The Final Five ☆

To make the Olympic team, Simone would have to compete at the Olympic **trials** in San Jose, California. If she did well, she could be chosen for the team. For Simone, being part of the Olympic team was the most important thing—more important than winning.

Simone was nervous to compete against gymnasts who had already won medals at the 2012 Olympics, but she didn't let her nerves stop her from doing her best. Simone won first place in the all-around, floor, and vault events. Then her biggest dream came true when Márta Károlyi chose her to be on the 2016 United States Olympic team! Simone's teammates would be Aly Raisman, Gabby Douglas, Laurie Hernandez, and Madison Kocian. Together, they called themselves the Final Five. They chose this name to honor Márta, who would be leading the Olympic team for the final time in 2016. It would also be the final year the Olympic team would have five members instead of four.

Even though teammates at the Olympics compete against each other for the highest scores and individual medals, they also compete as a group against other teams. As they prepared for the Olympics, Simone and her teammates became like sisters, supporting and cheering for each other. Simone hoped she could help the Final Five prove they were the best team in the world by earning the team gold medal.

> "The **team** comes **first**."

WHEN?

Simone graduates from high school.	Simone decides to delay college and go pro.	Simone makes the Olympic team.
2015	**2015**	**2016**

CHAPTER 6
THE OLYMPICS

Going for the Gold

At the end of July 2016, the Final Five and their coaches traveled to Rio de Janeiro, Brazil, for the Olympic Games. Athletes from over 200 countries would compete in more than 30 different sports. Simone and her teammates would be staying together in the Olympic Village. All the Olympic athletes would live and train in this specially built village for over two weeks. Simone loved it! It had training facilities such as gyms, tracks, and swimming pools. There were restaurants with every kind of food. After practice each day, Simone and her teammates relaxed, watched TV, and danced on their balcony. Best of all, Simone met famous athletes she had admired for years.

The gymnastics competitions would take place over six days. Simone's parents and sister traveled to Rio to watch and cheer for Simone.

Knowing her family was nearby kept Simone feeling confident and calm.

The Final Five started the competition by winning the team gold. Then Simone won gold medals for the individual all-around competition and vault. She came in third on the beam, winning a bronze medal. The floor routine was Simone's last event. The whole world watched as she performed a near-perfect routine, winning her fourth gold medal and setting new Olympic records!

At the end of the Olympics, there was a big closing ceremony to honor the athletes. Simone was chosen to carry the American flag for **Team USA**. At only 4 feet, 8 inches tall, Simone worried that she might not be able to hold the giant flag, which was twice her height. But she took the challenge and proudly led Team USA.

Taking a Break

After the Olympics, Simone was called the greatest gymnast of all time. She decided to take some time off from gymnastics to rest and have new experiences. Simone and her teammates toured the country for television interviews. They got to hang out with President Obama at the White House! Simone appeared in commercials, in magazines, and even on cereal boxes.

Simone was not competing in gymnastics, but she did enter another competition.

MYTH & FACT

MYTH: Gymnastics events are scored from 1 to 10.

FACT: In 2006, the scoring system changed. Gymnasts now earn up to 10 points for performance plus a difficulty score with no upper limit.

She showed off her dancing skills on the TV show *Dancing with the Stars*. She and her dance partner didn't win, but she had a great time.

Simone felt that the biggest reason her Olympic dreams had come true was because so many people had supported her. She wanted to give back by supporting others who were in need. She and her family **volunteered** to hand

JUMP IN THE THINK TANK

Simone took a break from gymnastics but stayed busy doing things she enjoyed. What do you like to do in your free time?

out clothing and supplies to people whose homes were damaged by a hurricane. She spoke to kids around the country about healthy living. She helped raise money for the **Special Olympics**, an event for athletes with **intellectual disabilities**. Simone also wrote a book about her life. She wanted her story to inspire others to follow their dreams.

WHEN?

2016 — Simone wins four Olympic gold medals.

2016 — Simone's book is published.

2017 — Simone competes on *Dancing with the Stars*.

CHAPTER 7

THE GREATEST GYMNAST

☆ A New Goal ☆

After more than a year off, Simone was ready to begin training again. Coach Aimee had moved to Florida, so Simone had to find a new coach. She began working with Laurent Landi. Every muscle hurt after her first days of training. Within a few weeks, the training routine began to feel normal again.

In 2018, Simone made a big comeback by breaking more national and world records. After her fifth world championship win in Germany in 2019, Simone had won 25 world medals, more

than any gymnast in history. That year, she also showed off a new move in her floor exercise. It was the fourth move to be named after her. Simone's original moves are known as the Biles floor, the Biles vault, the Biles beam, and now the Biles II floor. They are all among the most difficult moves ever performed in gymnastics.

Simone's new goal was the 2020 Olympics, which would be held in Tokyo, Japan. She was 23 years old and continued to train every day, practicing more and more difficult routines. She knew she could win a spot on the United States Olympic team and set new records in Tokyo.

MYTH & FACT

MYTH: The Olympic Games had never been moved or canceled before Tokyo 2020.

FACT: The 1916 Summer Olympics were canceled due to World War I. The 1940 and 1944 games were canceled because of World War II.

But nothing went as planned for Simone or any athlete that year. A terrible **pandemic** made people sick all over the world. The Olympic organizers decided to move the 2020 games to 2021. Simone was disappointed, but she knew it was the right decision. Now she would have a decision of her own to make.

Moving Forward

Simone had planned to **retire** from gymnastics after the 2020 Olympics. She wanted to take a break and do all the things she had missed out

on during her years of training. She could still retire, but it would mean missing the Olympics. Competing in the Olympics would mean another difficult year of training. In 2021, Simone would be 24 years old. Most gymnasts are in their best shape when they're teenagers. Simone thought about an extra year of training. It would be a lot of hard work. She believed she was strong enough to do it, but she also knew it would be a huge challenge.

JUMP IN THE THINK TANK

Leaders must often make big decisions that affect many people. What are some reasons a decision might be the right one, even if it makes some people unhappy?

Simone decided that she was not ready to give up on Tokyo. She would continue to train for her next challenge: Tokyo 2021! She wasn't sure what the year would hold, but she was determined to stay positive and do her best.

Simone works hard and never gives up, even when things get difficult. She has broken gymnastics records and won Olympic gold medals. She is the greatest gymnast of all time!

WHEN?

2018	2019	2020	2021
Simone returns to gymnastics after taking time off.	Simone wins her 25th world medal.	The Tokyo Olympics are postponed.	The new date of the Tokyo Olympics.

CHAPTER 8

SO . . . WHO IS SIMONE BILES?

Challenge Accepted!

Now that you know so much about Simone's inspiring life and success, let's test your knowledge in this who, what, when, where, why, and how quiz. Feel free to look back in the text to find the answers if you need to, but try to remember first!

1 Where was Simone born?

→ A Spring, Texas

→ B Chicago, Illinois

→ C Columbus, Ohio

→ D Detroit, Michigan

2 Who was Simone's coach from age eight through the 2016 Olympics?

→ A Adria Biles

→ B Gabby Douglas

→ C Aimee Boorman

→ D Mary Lou Retton

3 **Which gymnastics event was the most difficult for Simone?**

→ A Floor

→ B Uneven bars

→ C Vault

→ D Beam

4 **Why did Simone choose to be homeschooled?**

→ A She wanted more time for gymnastics training.

→ B She was doing poorly in public school.

→ C She hated her school.

→ D School isn't important for an athlete.

5 **What was Simone's first pet?**

→ A Guinea pig

→ B German shepherd dog

→ C Siamese cat

→ D Goldfish

6 **How tall is Simone?**

→ A 5 feet, 1 inch

→ B 4 feet, 2 inches

→ C 5 feet, 7 inches

→ D 4 feet, 8 inches

7 **When and where did Simone compete in her first Olympic Games?**

→ A 2012 in London, England

→ B 2016 in Rio de Janeiro, Brazil

→ C 2016 in Los Angeles, California

→ D 2020 in Tokyo, Japan

8 **What was Simone's team called at the 2016 Olympics?**

→ A The Fab Four

→ B The Final Five

→ C The Greatest of All Time

→ D The Károlyi Five

9 **How many medals did Simone win at the 2016 Olympics?**

→ A Two gold, two silver, one bronze

→ B Six gold

→ C One gold, four silver

→ D Four gold, one bronze

10 **Why is Simone a role model for all young people?**

→ A She proved that homeschooling is better than regular school.

→ B She showed how sports can make you rich.

→ C She was the fastest female runner of all time.

→ D She showed that if you work hard and believe in yourself, you can succeed.

Answers: 1. C, 2. C, 3. B, 4. A, 5. B, 6. D, 7. B, 8. B, 9. D, 10. D

Our World

Simone is one of the greatest athletes of all time. Let's look at some of the ways her accomplishments have helped shape our world today.

- Only men were allowed to compete in the first Olympic Games. Soon, women could compete in certain events, such as sailing, tennis, and golf. Women did not want to be told that there were sports they could not participate in. Athletes like Simone, and many before her, proved that women can excel in every sport.
- Many children live with both parents. Some live with one parent or other relatives. Some live with foster parents when their birth parents are unable to care for them. Simone lived in foster care before her grandparents became her parents. She is an example of how any kind of family can be happy when there is love and support.
- Role models come in many forms. Some help others and keep people safe, like teachers, firefighters, and nurses. Others pave the way to freedom and human rights. Successful athletes like Simone are often seen as role models because they show that there is no limit to what people can do when they pursue their dreams.

JUMP -IN THE- THINK TANK FOR MORE!

Let's think a little more about what Simone Biles has done and how her success has affected the way we see our world.

- → How does Simone's story encourage you to follow your dreams?
- → Why was Simone willing to give up a normal social life in order to achieve her goals?
- → How did Simone and her teammates support each other? How can you support friends who are trying to do their best?

Glossary

ADHD (attention deficit hyperactivity disorder): A condition in which a person has trouble paying attention and focusing, controlling certain behaviors, or both

adopted: To be legally made the child of someone who is not your birth parent

agility: The ability to move quickly and easily

all-around: A gymnastics competition in which gymnasts compete in all gymnastics events. The women's all-around competition has four events: vault, uneven bars, balance beam, and floor exercise.

athlete: A person who is trained in or good at sports, games, or exercises that require physical skill and strength

balance: The ability to move or to remain in a position without losing control or falling

balance beam: A narrow wooden beam on which gymnasts perform

championship: An important contest that decides which player or team is the best

college: A school of higher learning that is often attended after high school

compete: To try to win against others who are also trying to win

competition: A contest in which people try to win by being better than others at a certain skill or event

education: Formal schooling

elite: At the top level of a skill or sport

flexibility: The ability to bend and move easily

floor exercise: A series of dancing, leaping, and tumbling skills performed on an open floor

foster care: A temporary home for children who are unable to live with their birth parents

gymnast: A person who is trained or skilled in gymnastics

gymnastics: A sport in which athletes perform physical exercises on a mat or on special equipment

homeschooled: Taught at home instead of at a school

intellectual disabilities: Limitations that cause a person to learn and develop more slowly

junior elite: A top-level gymnast under the age of 16

leotard: A one-piece outfit that fits closely and is often worn by gymnasts and dancers

Olympics: Athletic games held every four years, each time in a different country. Athletes from many nations compete.

pandemic: An outbreak of a disease that spreads very quickly and affects many people throughout the world

poverty: The state in which people do not have enough money or other resources to meet their needs

professional: A person being paid for a certain skill

promote: To support or to try to sell by advertising

retire: To stop working in a certain career

routine: A performance by a gymnast in one event

senior elite: A top-level gymnast who is older than 15. Senior elites can compete in competitions around the world.

Special Olympics: A competition for athletes with different abilities, including intellectual disabilities

sports psychologist: An expert who helps athletes deal with thoughts and feelings so they can perform better

Team USA: All the athletes who represent the United States at the Olympics

title: A first-place position in a championship

training: Preparing for an athletic competition through practice and exercise

trials: A contest to decide who will compete in a later competition

uneven bars: An event in which gymnasts perform on two bars, one high and one low

vault: An event in which gymnasts launch from a springboard into the air

volunteer: To spend time working for a cause without being paid

world championship: A sports contest in which people or teams from many nations compete

Bibliography

Biles, Simone. *Courage to Soar: A Body in Motion, A Life in Balance*. Grand Rapids, MI: Zondervan, 2018.

Burns, Kylie. *Simone Biles: Gold Medal Gymnast and Advocate for Healthy Living*. New York: Crabtree Publishing Company, 2018.

Fishman, Jon M. *Simone Biles*. Minneapolis: Lerner Publications, 2017.

Mortensen, Lori. *Simone Biles: Gymnastics Star*. North Mankato, MN: Capstone Press, 2018.

"Simone Biles." *Biography.com*, A&E Networks Television. March 2, 2020. biography.com/athlete/simone-biles.

"Simone Biles." *International Olympic Committee*. Accessed March 10, 2020. olympic.org/simone-biles.

"USA Gymnastics: Simone Biles." *USA Gymnastics / Simone Biles*. Accessed March 22, 2020. usagym.org/pages/athletes/athleteListDetail.html?id=164887.

Acknowledgments

Thank you to the "Greatest of All Time," Simone Biles, for her inspiring dedication to gymnastics (my favorite Olympic event). Hats off to all the athletes who sacrifice a "normal life" in order to excel in their sports. I also would like to acknowledge the Olympic hopefuls whose dreams were disrupted by the postponement of the 2020 Olympics due to the pandemic. Many thanks to my editor, Kristen, for her support through this project, and to the entire Callisto Media team. Finally, a special shout-out to my talented writers' group, the Yentas—Margery, Karen, Tara, Laurie, Paula, and Corey—for your endless insights, encouragement, and friendship.

—R.B.

About the Author

RACHELLE BURK writes fiction and nonfiction for children ages 3 to 13. Her works include picture books *Don't Turn the Page!*, *Tree House in a Storm*, *The Best Four Questions* (a PJ Library selection), the award-winning biography *Painting in the Dark: Esref Armagan, Blind Artist*, and *20 Fearless Feminists: A Children's Book Celebrating Bold Women*. Her chapter book *The Tooth Fairy Trap* has been a One School/One Book choice, and her middle-grade science adventure novel *The Walking Fish* is a National Science Teachers Association award winner. Rachelle has written for numerous children's magazines, including *Scholastic Science World*, *Scholastic SuperScience*, *Scholastic Scope*, and *Highlights*. She is the founder of the writer's resource site ResourcesForChildrensWriters.com. A retired social worker, Rachelle is also a children's entertainer (Tickles the Clown and Mother Goof Storyteller). When she's not writing, Rachelle enjoys adventure travel, scuba diving, hiking, and caving. You can find out more about her books and school visits at **RachelleBurk.com**.

About the Illustrator

STEFFI WALTHALL is an illustrator and character designer who has always been inspired by strong, fearless women, whether in history or in fiction. Steffi loves human-centric stories and creating images that celebrate and embrace diversity (and usually include a lady with a sword). When not working on a project, she can be found searching for inspiration in a book or out in nature with her Polaroid camera looking for another story to begin.

WHO WILL INSPIRE YOU NEXT?

EXPLORE A WORLD OF HEROES AND ROLE MODELS IN ***THE STORY OF...*** BIOGRAPHY SERIES FOR NEW READERS.

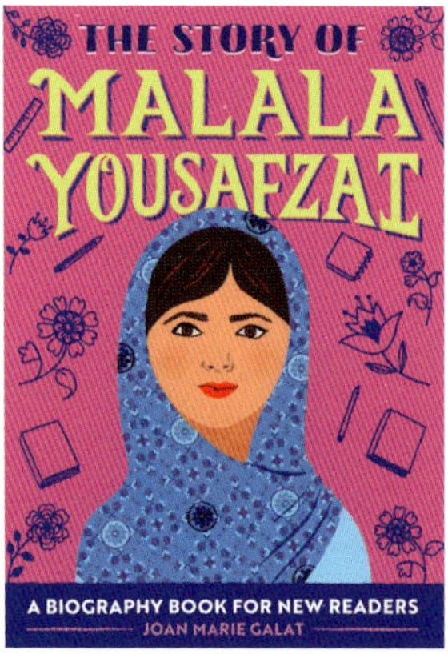

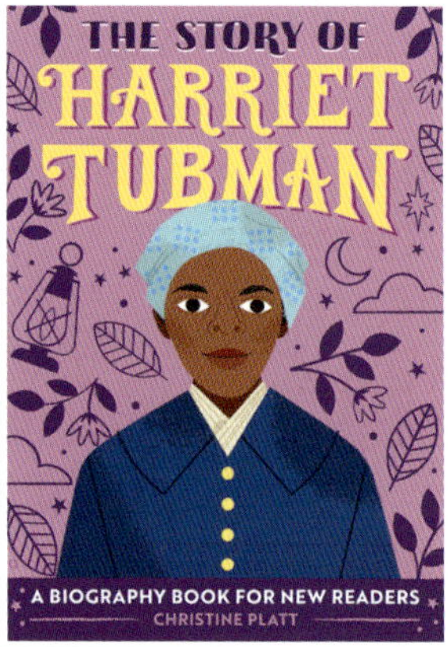

LOOK FOR THIS SERIES
WHEREVER BOOKS AND EBOOKS ARE SOLD

Alexander Hamilton
Albert Einstein
Abraham Lincoln
George Washington
Jane Goodall
Barack Obama
Helen Keller
Marie Curie